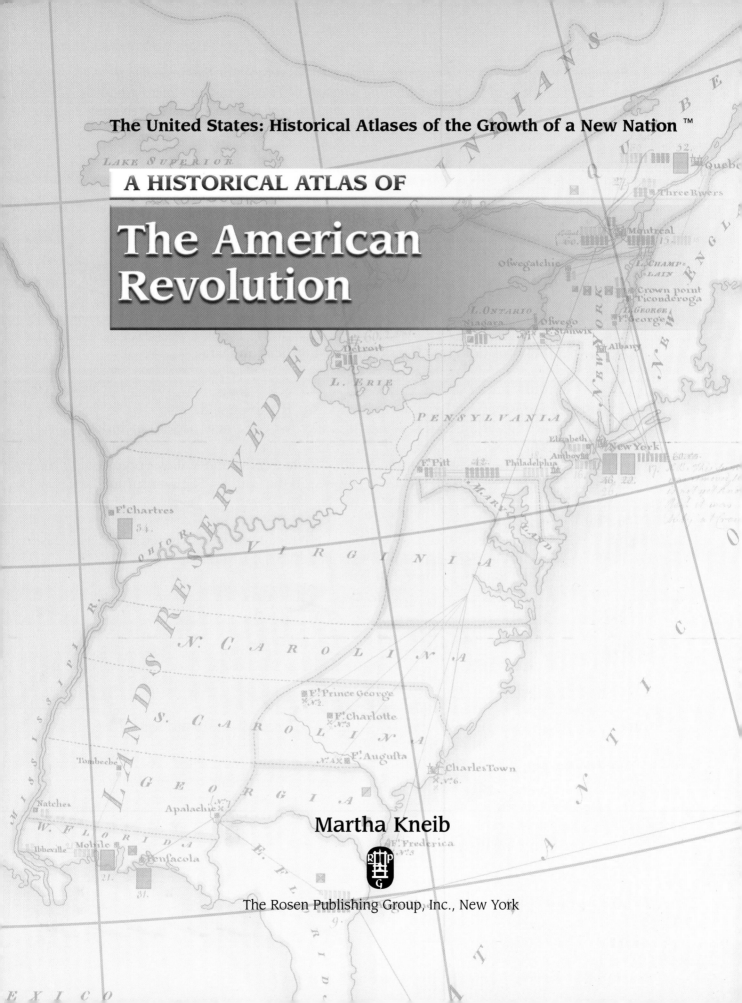

The United States: Historical Atlases of the Growth of a New Nation ™

A HISTORICAL ATLAS OF
The American Revolution

Martha Kneib

The Rosen Publishing Group, Inc., New York

To Benjamin Washburn of the Continental army, who was present for the surrender at Yorktown; to David Roberts of the Vermont militia who was at Ticonderoga and later witnessed Burgoyne's defeat at Saratoga; and to Joseph Barutel dit Toulouse, who volunteered to go with George Rogers Clark to Vincennes in February 1779

Published in 2005 by The Rosen Publishing Group, Inc.
29 East 21st Street, New York, NY 10010

Copyright © 2005 by The Rosen Publishing Group, Inc.

First Edition

Library of Congress Cataloging-in-Publication Data

Kneib, Martha
A historical atlas of the American Revolution/by Martha Kneib.–1st ed.
  p. cm—(The United States, historical atlases of the growth of a new nation) Includes
  bibliographical references and index.
Contents: Early losses—The tide turns in the North—Philadelphia and Valley Forge—
The war on the frontier—The war on the sea—The war in the South—The war turned
upside down.
ISBN 1-4042-0204-8
1. United States—History—Revolution, 1775–1783—Juvenile literature. 2. United
States—History—Revolution, 1775–1783—Maps for children. [1. United States—
History— Revolution, 1775–1783—Maps. 2. Atlases.]
I. Title. II. Series.
E208.K63 2004
973.3–dc22
2003069312

Manufactured in the United States of America

On the cover: Top: A portrait of George Washington in 1796 as commander in chief of the Continental army by Gilbert Stuart. Bottom: A painting by H. Charles McBarron Jr., depicting the Battle of Guilford Court House on March 15, 1781. Background: A map of the eastern coast of North America illustrating encampments of British soldiers prior to the Revolutionary War in 1766.

Contents

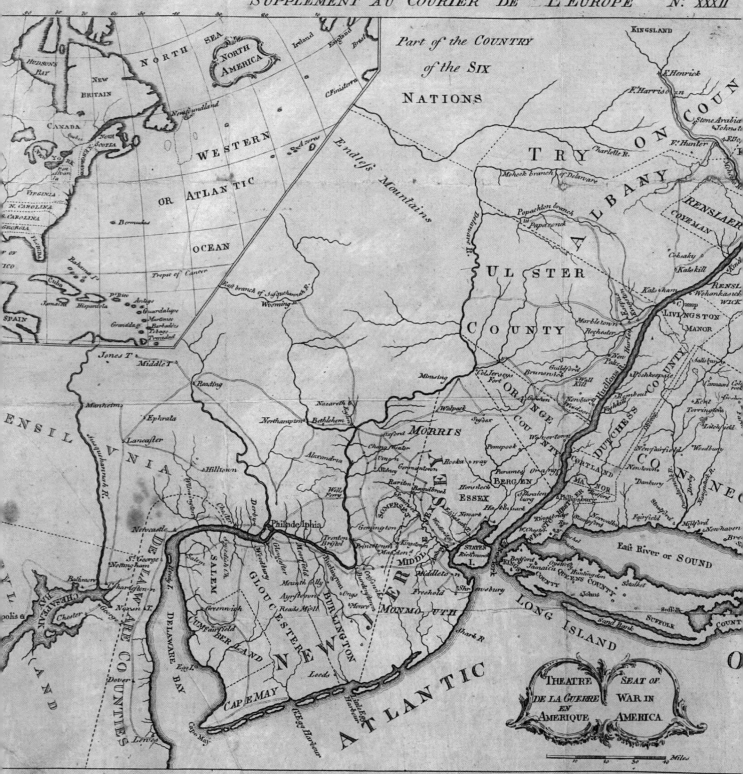

Part of the COUNTRY of the SIX NATIONS

NORTH AMERICA

NORTH SEA

Ireland
England
C. Finisterra

HUDSON'S BAY
NEW BRITAIN
CANADA
NOVA SCOTIA
Newfoundland
Azores
Bermudas

WESTERN OR ATLANTIC OCEAN

Tropic of Cancer

NEW YORK
VIRGINIA
N. CAROLINA
S. CAROLINA
FLORIDA
Bahama I.
Cuba
Jamaica
Hispaniola
Antigo
Guardaloupe
Martinico
Barbadoes
Tobago
Trinidad
Granada I.
SPAIN
MEXICO
P.to Rico

Endless Mountains

KINGSLAND
F. Henrick
F. Harrison
Stone Arabia
Johnstn
E. Stn.
Charlotte R.

TRY ON COUNTY
ALBANY
Mohock branch of Delaware
Popachton branch
Papacock

RENSLAER
COYEMAN
Coksaky
Kalskill
Katsham
RENSL
Wohankashick WICK
Camp
LIVINGSTON MANOR
Salisbury
Canaan
Geo.ho
Kent
Torrington
Litchfield

ULSTER COUNTY
Marbletown
Rochester
Guildford
Brunswick
Wall Kill
New Paltz
Newburgh
Windsor
Hurley
Kingsbury
DUCHESS COUNTY
Poughkeepsie
Fishkill
Newfairfield
Newtown
Danbury
CONNEC

ORANGE COUNTY
Col. Jerseys Fort
Goshen
Wolverton
Pomapeck
Orange
Paramus
BERGEN
Hackinsack
CORTLAND MANOR
Peekskill
Shraltenburg
W. Chester
E. Chester
Phillipsburg
Bedford
Stanford
Norwalk
Fairfield
Millford
Newhaven
Bre

Minsing
Walpack
Sussex
Oxford
Chang Water
Unpn
Sidney
MORRIS
Rockaway
Germantown
Raritan
Boundbrook
SOMERSET
ESSEX
Newark
Horsneck
Elizabeth
Wodbridge
Amboy

Manheim
Reading
Nazareth
Northampton
Bethlehem
Alexandria
Hilltown
Ephrata
Lancaster

PENSILVANIA
Susquehannah R.
Pittsburgh
Chester
Darby
Newcastle
DELAWARE
Wilmington
St. George
Nottingham
Baltimore
Charlestown
Georgetown
MARYLAND
Chester
Annapolis
CHESAPEAK

Philadelphia
Trenton
Bristol
Princetown
Macdens
Kingston
Gennington
Wells Ferry
JERSEY
NEW JERSEY
STATEN I.
Richmond
York
KINGS COUNTY
Bedford
Oyster B.
Jamaica
QUEEN'S COUNTY
Huntington
Setalket
Johns
SUFFOLK COUNTY

MIDDLE
Middleton
Freehold
Shrewsbury
MONMOUTH
Shark R.

East River or SOUND

LONG ISLAND
Sand Bank

SALEM
CUMBERLAND
Greenwich
Fairfield
GLOUCESTER
Woodbury
Moorfield
Meunth
Ayrstown
Reads M.
BURLINGTON
Mount Holly
Ongs
Monro
Leeds
Bordentown
Recklestown

DELAWARE BAY
Egg I.
Jones T.
Middle T.
Dover
Lewes
CAPE MAY
Cape May
Little Egg Harbour
G. Egg Harbour

NEW JERSEY

ATLANTIC

East branch of Susquehannah R.
Wyoming

THEATRE DE LA GUERRE EN AMERIQUE
SEAT OF WAR IN AMERICA

10   20   30   40   Miles

71-5448

[London, 1777]

INTRODUCTION

The first shots of the Revolutionary War were fired at Lexington, Massachusetts, on April 19, 1775. By that time, war between England and its American colonies had been on the horizon for a long time. The American colonists had been arguing with England for years. Many of them decided that they wanted independence.

In 1763, England's King George III and his ministers discovered that their country was bankrupt. England needed to find more sources of revenue. King George's immediate solution was to tax the American colonists. However, he and the rest of England were unprepared for the storm of protest from across the Atlantic Ocean. The tension quickly escalated. In 1770, British

A detail of the New England colonies is pictured on this 1777 map that depicts the "Theater of War in America." The majority of the fighting between British and American forces took place in the northeastern section of the United States. The British hoped to divide the colonies in order to gain the upper hand in the war, while American forces tried and failed to take over Canada. Before the end of the war in 1783, France, Spain, and the Netherlands would also be involved in the conflict.

Paul Revere created this engraving of the tragic shootings in 1770 known as the Boston Massacre. Eight uniformed soldiers (right) fire at a group of civilians (left), as three other civilians lay bleeding on the ground. Behind the British troops is a row of buildings including the Royal Customs House, which bears the sign "Butcher's Hall." Five patriots died in the incident, which further provoked alarm among the colonists. Underneath the engraving are eighteen lines of verse, beginning, "Unhappy Boston! [S]ee thy sons deplore, thy hallowed Walks besmeared with guiltless Gore."

soldiers fatally shot five people in a tragic event that became known as the Boston Massacre.

Colonists refused to pay the taxes, such as those on imported sugar (Molasses Act, 1733), printed articles (Stamp Act, 1765), and paper, glass, china, and paint (Townshend Duties, 1767). They boycotted British goods such as wool and tea. In England, thousands of people were forced out of work due to the boycotts. Tea consumption in the colonies dropped by 75 percent in less than three years.

In 1773, about fifty members of the Sons of Liberty (an organization that formed in 1765 to oppose the Stamp Act) boarded three British ships in Boston Harbor that were filled with tea. They dumped 342 chests of tea into the harbor, costing the British about £10,000 ($18,157). In response to what became known as the Boston Tea Party, the British government closed the port of Boston and passed five acts known as the Intolerable (Coercive) Acts. These new laws kept colonial ports closed until imported British cargo was completely paid, ensuring no further financial losses for the British.

On September 5, 1774, the First Continental Congress met in Philadelphia to protest the taxes

ADVERTISEMENT.

THE Members of the Aſſociation of the Sons of Liberty, are requeſted to meet at the City-Hall, at one o'Clock, To-morrow, (being Friday) on Buſineſs of the utmoſt Importance ;—And every other Friend to the Liberties, and Trade of America, are hereby moſt cordially invited, to meet at the ſame Time and Place.   *The Committee of the Aſſociation.*

Thurſday, NEW-YORK, 16th December, 1773.

This newspaper advertisement from December 16, 1773, calls for a meeting in New York City of the Sons of Liberty. The Sons were a group of patriots opposed to the Stamp Act. They formed in 1765 to peacefully oppose British legislation through petitions and assemblies. Both Paul Revere and Samuel Adams were members of the Sons of Liberty.

brought on them by the British. All of the colonies except Georgia were represented. Many men who would later be a part of the Revolution, such as George Washington and John Adams, attended the First Continental Congress. At this time, the colonists were not yet considering war. They instead adopted a Declaration of Rights and Grievances. King George was angered by the declaration and refused to repeal the new taxes. Now that the king had refused to negotiate, many colonists feared that the problems between the colonies and England would worsen. Before long, many Americans started to stockpile weapons and ammunition.

The following year, on April 18, 1775, British troops in Boston were taken away from their normal duties. Their exit from Boston, though taken under cover of darkness, was keenly observed. Dr. Joseph Warren, a physician, writer, and supporter of the Revolution, witnessed their movement. Warren sent out two riders, William Dawes and Paul Revere, to warn others. Revere established a signal with lanterns in the Old North Church, which alerted other riders to spread the news of the British troop movement.

Soon, news that the British were on their way reached Lexington and Concord, both in Massachusetts. Local militias assembled to block their path. On the morning of April 19, British troops and local militia faced each other over the village green at Lexington. Someone—no one ever knew who—fired the first shot. Eight of the militia died and ten were wounded. The militia retreated in the face of British fire. The war had begun.

CHAPTER ONE
Early Losses

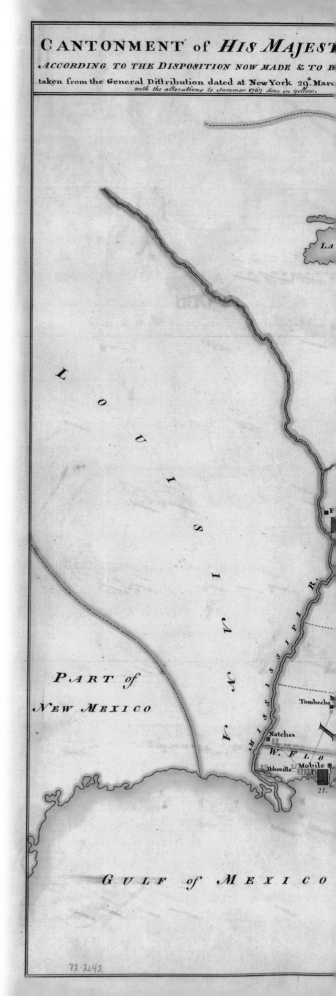

CANTONMENT of *HIS MAJEST*
ACCORDING TO THE DISPOSITION NOW MADE & TO B
taken from the General Diftribution dated at New York 29. Mar
with the alterations to Summer 1767 done in yellow.

The Americans were not prepared for a lengthy war. When militia from other states rallied to the aid of Massachusetts, the president of Harvard University saved them from hunger by offering them food from its storage lockers. At this time, the colonies had no organized army, only groups of ill-trained and ill-fed men who had few supplies.

Still they had the will to fight, and so did the Second Continental Congress, which met on May 10, 1775. That same day, Ethan Allen and his Green Mountain Boys (a militia from Vermont) captured Fort Ticonderoga in New York. Although Allen claimed to be acting on behalf of the Continental Congress, they had had no warning of his actions. A few men in Congress even debated returning the fort to the British

British military bases and detachments are visible in this map of the eastern half of the United States. Created by Daniel Patterson for British officials in 1767, the map details the movements of British forces and labels the frontier as "Land Reserved for the Indians." Because Native Americans viewed the British as less of a threat to their well-being than the colonists, many of them fought on the British side during the Revolutionary War.

as no official declaration of war had yet been made.

But events were moving too quickly to schedule such a debate. On May 12, colonists took Crown Point, another fort located in New York. A third fort, St. Johns in Quebec, was also taken but abandoned by the Americans and later reoccupied by the British.

The Battle of Bunker Hill

Congress authorized the formation of a Continental army on June 14, 1775, and appointed George Washington as its commander in chief. Before Washington could form an army or train anyone, another battle took place. This was the Battle of Bunker Hill.

Outside the city of Boston lay several hills that overlooked the town. Word came to the Americans that the British intended to occupy these heights. To prevent this, the Americans fortified the top of Breed's Hill, a location closer to the city than Bunker Hill. On the morning of June 17, a British ship fired upon the Americans. British troops were sent up Breed's Hill and were repulsed by massed musket fire. On the third assault, the British got up the hill and finished the battle with bayonets.

The Americans suffered about 440 casualties, one of whom was Joseph Warren, the patriot who had witnessed the British soldiers leaving for Lexington and Concord. The British defeated the Americans but lost more than 1,000 soldiers. The Americans had proven that untrained men could do well under fire from a superior, well-trained force. Despite the defeat, the Americans were encouraged by the bravery of their militia.

The British couldn't keep Boston, however. By March 1776, the American militia had dragged the guns captured at Ticonderoga to sites overlooking the city, and their forces had swelled. For the first time, the Americans outnumbered the British, who ended up evacuating Boston on St. Patrick's Day.

Part of the American fervor for the cause of independence was incited by a popular pamphlet, *Common Sense.* Printed a few months earlier by Thomas Paine, an English printer who had recently moved to the colonies, it called for colonists to rise up against the British. *Common Sense* urged Americans to

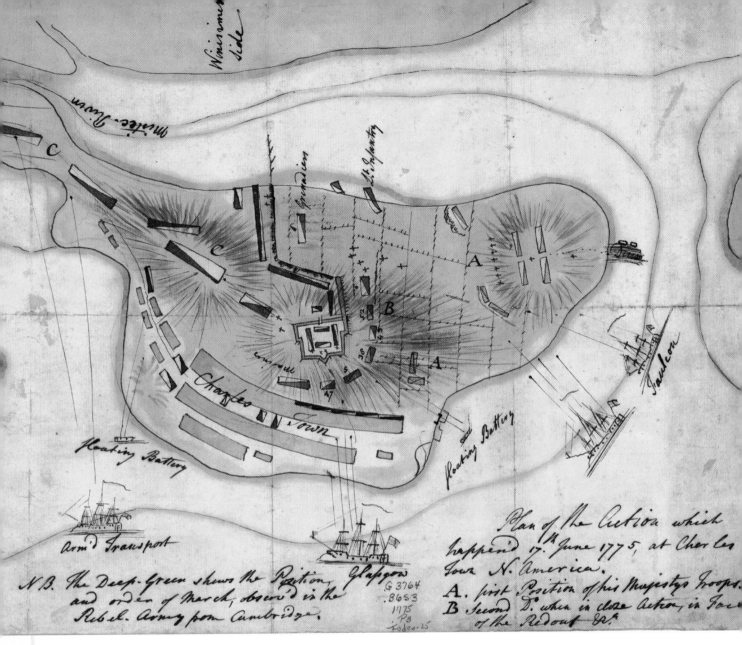

This American map details the actions of British troops during the Battle of Bunker Hill, which took place on June 17, 1775. The early battle was an important American victory that inspired the patriot cause. Swift movements by American forces gave them the upper hand in the campaign, which killed or injured more than 1,000 British soldiers. Approximately 440 Americans also lost their lives in the battle, but the unexpected victory fueled their spirit.

develop a republic—a democratic government without a king.

The March to Canada

Fearing a British invasion from the north that summer, two American expeditions were sent out to drive the British from Canada. However, without orders, Ethan Allen attempted to take Montreal on his own. He had been captured, and now the British were prepared for future attacks. General Richard Montgomery, in charge of one of the

American units, also made his way toward Montreal. The British defense slowed his advance. The other American unit, under the command of Benedict Arnold, marched through present-day Maine but was halted by a storm that kept them from crossing the St. Lawrence River. Arnold's force could not reach Quebec before British reinforcements arrived in the city.

The two American units met on December 2 and faced the prospect of a winter siege, but they could not delay for long. On the night of December 31, the Americans attacked. General Montgomery was killed. Arnold was wounded in the left leg and forced to retreat.

In the summer of 1776, the British attempted to invade from Canada

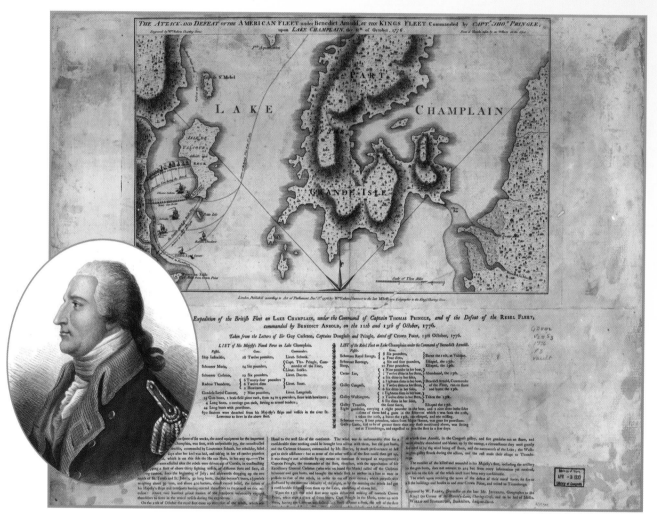

This map recounts the expedition of British general Guy Carleton's fleet on Lake Champlain and the defeat of the American fleet under Benedict Arnold on October 11, 1776. Arnold (1741–1801, *inset*) contributed greatly to early American successes. However, he was passed over for a military promotion. In 1779, Arnold became the Revolutionary War's most famous traitor when he offered his services to the British. A monument to his left leg (which was injured twice while he served the American cause) can today be found on the grounds of the Saratoga National Historic Park in New York.

but Arnold built ships on Lake Champlain to stop them. The British were forced to disassemble their ships on the St. Lawrence River and carry the pieces overland to the lake for reconstruction. Despite the delay, the British won the resulting naval battle and American ships were destroyed. However, the campaign on the lake had taken so much time that the British had to return to Canada before winter. Arnold had sacrificed his ships, but suspended the invasion.

A Declaration of Independence

The summer of 1776 was momentous for another reason. Congress declared the United States "free and independent" on July 2, the same day that redcoats landed in Staten Island, New York. Congress further resolved that colonists were "absolved from all allegiance to the British Crown." On July 4, Congress adopted the Declaration of Independence, written by Thomas Jefferson, John Adams, and Benjamin Franklin. The declaration accused King George of trying to destroy government in the colonies by his use of excessive force.

The British forces delayed action for some time during 1776 while waiting for the arrival of additional troops. Finally, in late summer,

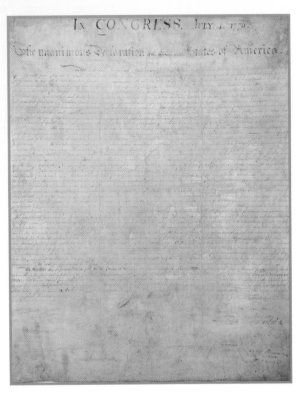

The Second Continental Congress adopted the Declaration of Independence, written by Thomas Jefferson, on July 4, 1776. Its inspiration for all Americans is as powerful today as it was in 1776: "We hold these truths to be self-evident: That all men are created equal; that they are endowed by their Creator with certain unalienable rights; that among these are life, liberty, and the pursuit of happiness."

General William Howe, a British commander with American sympathies, advanced on Long Island. Twenty thousand British troops, mostly German mercenaries called Hessians, landed south of the American positions. Facing this large force were about 17,000 Americans in the Continental army, few of them trained. General Washington marched his army south from Boston to defend New York. On August 27, the advancing British troops

George Washington (1732–1799, *left*) was commissioned as a lieutenant colonel during the French and Indian War (1754–1763). Washington was nominated in 1775 as the commander in chief of the Continental army. In 1789, he was elected the first president of the United States, a position he held until 1797. Hostility and mental illness marked the reign of King George III (1738–1820, *right*), British monarch during the time of the American Revolution. His refusal to end the conflict in 1776 proved foolish, and he subsequently lost power.

defeated the American militia after two significant losses, battles that took place at Brooklyn Heights and on Manhattan Island. The Americans suffered 1,300 casualties while the British lost fewer than 400 men. (At least 3,000 more Americans were captured in other engagements and became British prisoners. They spent the rest of the war trapped on British vessels anchored in New York Harbor, where most died from disease.)

Further losses in New York at Harlem Heights and Kip's Bay in September kept the Americans on the defensive. On November 16, the British took Fort Washington and all of its guns. The fight for New York was over. The British occupied the city for the rest of the Revolutionary War.

After the loss of New York, Washington and his remaining troops had been forced to retreat south into New Jersey. Even with the arrival of volunteers from Pennsylvania, Washington had only about 6,000 men under his command. Winter had set in, and British troops went on a rampage across the colony. They started fires, destroyed public buildings and churches, stole supplies, and killed or assaulted anyone in their path no matter if he or she was a British loyalist or a patriot.

Christmas in Trenton

It was December 1776, and the British assumed the fighting was over for the year. They quartered their troops by detachments. Washington knew this meant he could attack each group individually. However, no one on the British side felt the Americans had enough supplies, men, or boldness to make such a move.

The British were wrong. Angered by the loss of New York, Washington came up with a daring plan of attack. On Christmas Day, Washington led 2,500 men from the Continental army and 18 cannon toward Trenton to attack a Hessian encampment. The weather was bitterly cold. To make matters worse, it began to sleet just before midnight. The men were ferried across the

Delaware River, an operation that took more time than Washington had hoped. The weather delayed his arrival in Trenton until after dawn the next morning.

The delay did not matter. Because of the Christmas holiday, the Hessian unit had posted no sentries. Most of the soldiers were still sleeping after their hearty celebrations of the day before. Washington and his troops suddenly attacked, to the complete surprise of the Hessians.

The Hessians lost 50 men while another 900 were captured by the American troops. The Hessian commander, Colonel Johann Rall, was injured and later died. No Americans died, and only a few were injured, including James Monroe, who would later become the fifth president of the United States.

The one-sided victory at Trenton inspired the colonists and gave them new faith in General Washington. The British, by contrast, were stunned by their loss. General Howe immediately sent General Charles Cornwallis, whose life-long military career gave him an advantage over the Americans, to take command of the situation in New Jersey. Cornwallis marched on Washington's position. When he felt he had Washington trapped, he stopped for a rest. Cornwallis planned to destroy Washington's forces the next morning.

Instead of waiting in the trap overnight, Washington decided to flank the enemy, or attack them from both sides. He left 400 men behind with instructions to keep the campfires lit and slip away at dawn. The rest of the army moved as silently as possible toward Princeton. After daybreak, Lieutenant Colonel Charles Mawhood of the British army discovered his enemy behind him. Two skirmishes were fought, and no real victor appeared on the battlefield. The triumph lay in Washington's ability

British general Charles Cornwallis (1738–1805) is most often remembered for his surrender of British troops in Yorktown, Virginia, in 1781, which effectively ended the Revolutionary War. Cornwallis was also a British statesman who later became governor-general of British India in 1786. Although he was known to be in favor of the American colonists, he fought against them during the Revolution.

to get through Princeton with his army intact. Instead of being destroyed by Cornwallis's forces, the Americans lost roughly 100 men. Successes at Trenton and Princeton inspired volunteers to join the Continental army, including African American slaves who eventually won freedom in exchange for their duty.

Burgoyne's Campaign

In June 1777, the British tried once more to invade the colonies from Canada. Lieutenant General John Burgoyne was put in charge of the troops in Montreal. He marched them south, first sending them down Lake Champlain in canoes. British general Howe was ordered to meet with Burgoyne in a pincer movement. This is a maneuver that allows troops to attack from both sides and the front. However, Howe turned his attentions elsewhere. Although no one is certain why, Howe may have felt that Burgoyne's forces were more than

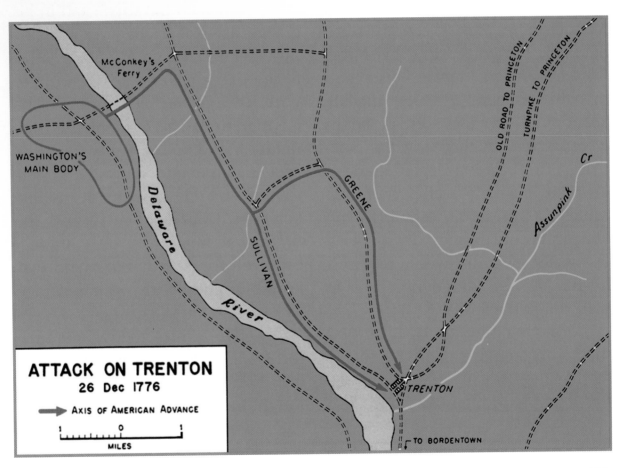

This map shows the approximate advance by General George Washington and his Continental army on British and Hessian soldiers in Trenton, New Jersey, in December 1776. Because Washington feared the British were about to attack Philadelphia, he and his army crossed the Delaware River during a storm and captured them by surprise. The patriots killed or wounded approximately 100 British and Hessian soldiers and captured 900 others. The battle was a major American victory and bolstered the patriot cause.

sufficient to destroy a few rebels in northern New York and that assistance from his troops would be unnecessary. Also, it is possible that some of his orders from London were delivered too late to have been effective. Burgoyne, therefore, was marching south under the belief that his troops would meet Howe's troops in New York. Burgoyne believed that he would have ample reinforcements. This never happened.

Burgoyne marched on to Fort Ticonderoga, and the American commander there, Major General Arthur St. Clair, recognized that his forces were insufficient to meet Burgoyne's in battle. General St. Clair quickly abandoned the fort. British hopes were inspired by this early, easy success. But Burgoyne then made a mistake. He had a choice of two routes to his next destination: an overland route through dense forest, or a water route that would require a longer journey. Burgoyne chose to go through the forest.

Local inhabitants had burned their crops and driven off their cattle so that the British could not forage for food. Patriot militias had also felled many trees, making the British journey even more difficult. The forest itself was so dense that Burgoyne's troops trekked only one mile (1.4 km) per day.

It wasn't until August that the British made it through the forest and met the Americans. The first engagement was at the Battle of Oriskany in New York, and the second at the Battle of Bennington, the first conflict in the Battles of Saratoga. By this time, the Americans knew exactly how many men Burgoyne had in his charge as well as their exact positions. By evening on August 16, most of the Canadian and Loyalist forces with Burgoyne had fled. His German units had attempted to surrender, though their message had been misunderstood by the Americans. All told, the Americans lost between 30 and 40 men, and the British had more than 900 wounded, captured, or killed. Burgoyne was now burdened with wounded men and limited supplies.

The two armies spent some time fortifying their positions and resting. On September 19, the forces fought the Battle of Freeman's Farm.

Lieutenant General John Burgoyne's campaign to Albany during the summer of 1777, which was cut short by patriot forces in Saratoga, New York, is seen on this map. Left with little ammunition, food, or other supplies, Burgoyne was forced to surrender to General Horatio Gates. Burgoyne (1722–1792, *inset*) was born in London and joined the British army in 1740. He had a melodramatic manner of speaking, which caused others to ridicule him. The Americans referred to him as Gentleman Johnny. However, his own men liked him, as he always looked out for their welfare. Burgoyne opposed cruel punishments, forbade his men to collect scalps or torture prisoners, and declared that women, children, and the aged should be unmolested.

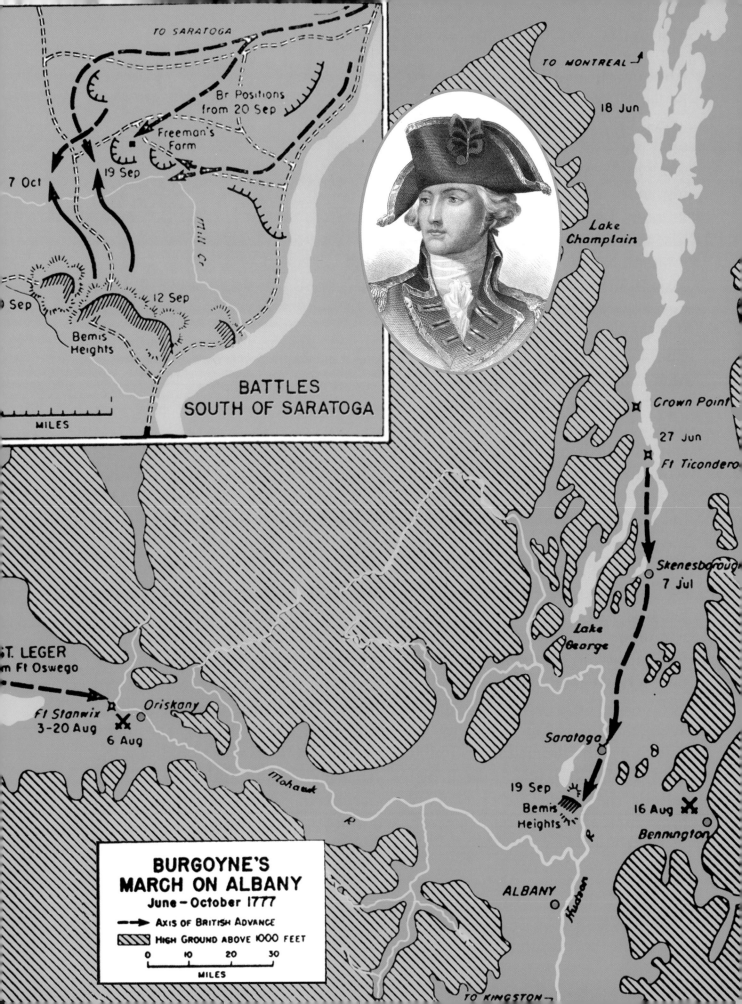

BATTLES SOUTH OF SARATOGA

TO SARATOGA

Br Positions from 20 Sep

Freeman's Farm

7 Oct

19 Sep

12 Sep

Mill Cr.

9 Sep

Bemis Heights

MILES

TO MONTREAL

18 Jun

Lake Champlain

Crown Point

27 Jun

Ft Ticonderoga

Skenesborough
7 Jul

Lake George

Saratoga

19 Sep

Bemis Heights

16 Aug

Bennington

ST. LEGER
m Ft Oswego

Ft Stanwix
3-20 Aug

Oriskany

6 Aug

Mohawk R.

ALBANY

Hudson R.

BURGOYNE'S MARCH ON ALBANY
June – October 1777

→ Axis of British Advance

High Ground above 1000 Feet

0   10   20   30

MILES

TO KINGSTON

Although Daniel Morgan and Benedict Arnold led the Americans brilliantly, the British won the day. British losses were high, with one unit losing more than 75 percent of its men. Burgoyne again had his troops build entrenchments and fortifications. It wasn't until October 7 that he faced the Americans again in the Battle of Bemis Heights. The British defended their new entrenchments bravely, but Benedict Arnold, placing himself between the American and British lines, led the Americans to victory. In the process, he suffered wounds to his left leg, but his heroism saved the day.

Burgoyne retreated, but he was surrounded. On October 17, 1777, he surrendered to the Americans at Saratoga. The American victory in the Battles of Saratoga turned the tide of the war and got the attention of France. The French were eager to avenge their earlier defeat by the British in the French and Indian War (1754–1763), which the British called the Seven Years' War. Previously, France had secretly

British general John Burgoyne surrenders to patriot general Horatio Gates in this engraving after the Battles of Saratoga on October 17, 1777. The battles were important for the colonists since their victory helped gain prompt attention from France, a nation that ultimately helped the American Revolutionary cause.

helped the Americans with supplies and money. After Saratoga, France openly supported the American cause. On February 6, 1778, a formal treaty of alliance was signed, and France recognized America as a new, independent nation. France also abandoned any claim to North American lands in Canada and U.S. territory east of the Mississippi River. France was now formally at war with Great Britain, a country that was now forced to fight on the American mainland and in the Caribbean, where both the French and British had colonies.

General Howe had not been idle while General Burgoyne was facing American forces in New York. After deciding that Burgoyne did not require his help, he and his troops moved on to Philadelphia. Howe's approach was slow, however, and General Washington was able to mount a defense of Philadelphia at nearby Brandywine. The Brandywine Creek itself was shallow and easy to cross, but the adjacent valley was steep. Assembling an infantry at the top of the valley would be difficult.

The Loss of Philadelphia

Washington's forces engaged Howe's forces on September 11, 1777, but were unaware that Howe had split his troops into two groups. One group flanked the Americans and surrounded Philadelphia on the north and west sides. Washington received mixed reports about these movements. Contradictory accounts kept Washington from mounting an adequate defense against Cornwallis's second column. Battles throughout the day resulted in at least 1,000 American casualties and 600 for the British. The Americans also lost eleven cannon and were forced to retreat. The battle was one of the largest land battles of the war, involving roughly 15,000 British and 11,000 American soldiers. It was also the only time

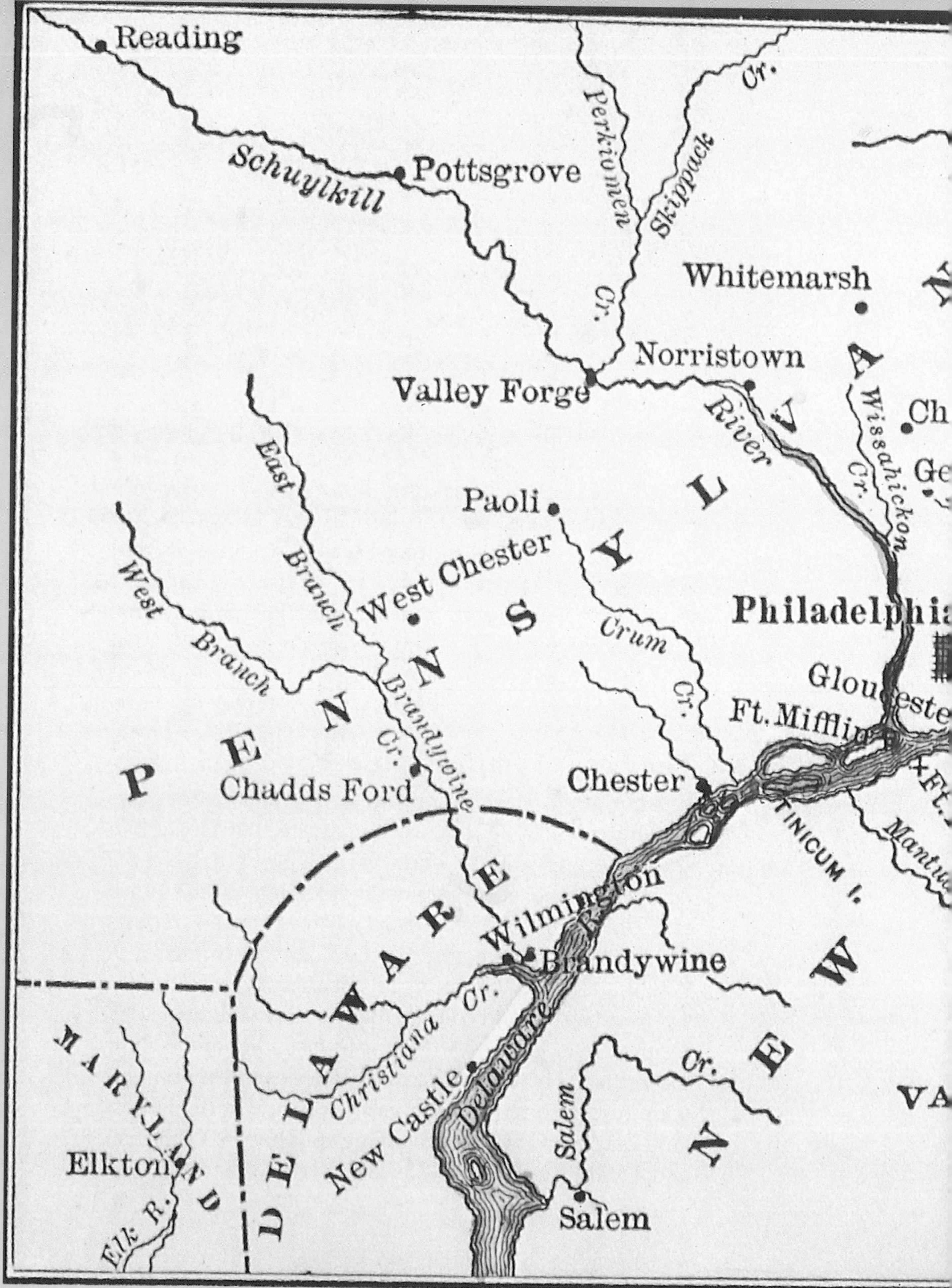

Reading

Schuylkill

Pottsgrove

Perkiomen Cr.

Skippack Cr.

Cr.

Whitemarsh

Norristown

Valley Forge

River

Wissahickon Cr.

Ch

Ge

Paoli

West Chester

PENNSYLVANIA

Crum Cr.

Philadelphia

East Branch

West Branch

Brandywine Cr.

Chadds Ford

Chester

Gloucester

Ft. Mifflin

Ft.

DELAWARE

Wilmington

Brandywine

TINICUM I.

Mantua

Christiana Cr.

New Castle

Delaware

MARYLAND

Elk R.

Elkton

Salem Cr.

NEW

Salem

VA

Cr.

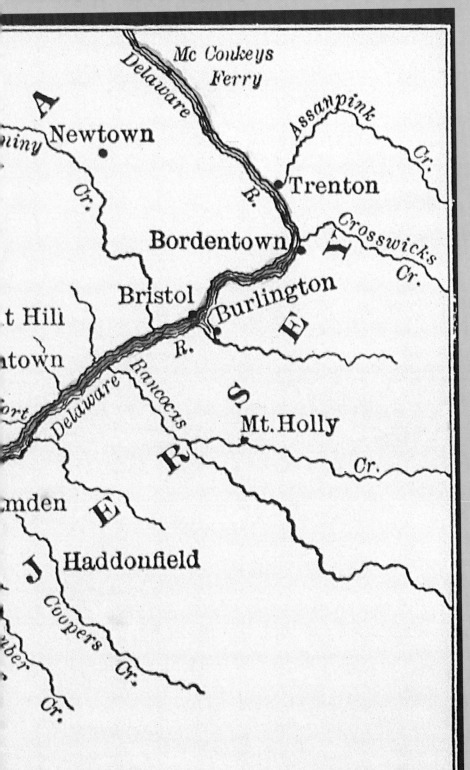

Mc Conkeys
Ferry

Delaware

A

Newtown

iny

Cr.

Assanpink

R.

Trenton

Cr.

Bordentown

Crosswicks

Cr.

Bristol

Burlington

t Hill

E

R.

S

town

Delaware

Rancocas

Mt. Holly

R

Fort

E

Cr.

mden

E

Coopers

Haddonfield

J

Cr.

ber Cr.

EY FORGE, PHILADELPHIA,
AND
BRANDYWINE.

Bormay & Co., N.Y.

This map shows eastern Pennsylvania, including Philadelphia, Valley Forge, and Brandywine. The west bank of the Schuylkill River where General George Washington and the Continental army established their quarters during the winter of 1777 to 1778 is also visible. The British occupied Philadelphia at the time, but Washington knew that he and his 11,000-man army could defend their position if discovered. Despite lack of food, inadequate clothing, and the bitter cold weather, the Continental army managed to emerge as a reorganized force by the following summer with the help of French allies.

that Washington and Howe fought head to head.

On September 26, the remaining British troops marched into Philadelphia, then the capital of the United States, and occupied the city. Having an enemy force occupy a nation's capital city often meant a war had been lost. American morale slipped.

Washington struck back at British troops in the Battle of Germantown. On October 4, he divided his forces into four groups and planned to attack at dawn. Although all four groups were late, and one got lost, the morning went well for the Americans. But eventually the lack of coordination between Washington's four groups, and the strong British defense, saved the day for the British. At one point, two of Washington's units were firing at each other in the confusion.

The battle was a loss for the Americans, though their spirits were high. They felt that the loss had been due to poor communications, rather than a lack of effort on the part of the soldiers. Cornwallis was impressed enough that he did not pursue the Americans, but instead retreated to Philadelphia. In Europe, Washington's ability to continually fight after the defeat at Brandywine impressed the French almost as much as if the Americans had won.

Winter at Valley Forge

Washington occupied heights overlooking the city and prevented Howe from foraging in the countryside for food. Several times, Howe sent out forces to try to lure Washington into a disastrous attack, but Washington wasn't tricked. Eventually, Howe gave up and settled into winter quarters in the city. Washington left the heights and went with his troops to establish a winter camp at Valley Forge, a site a few miles from Philadelphia that was simple to defend.

The Continental army spent six months at Valley Forge, the first three in extreme conditions. Some soldiers had no shoes and most had little food. The cold was bitter. The Marquis de Lafayette, a Frenchman who volunteered to fight alongside General Washington, wrote, "The unfortunate soldiers were in want of everything; they had neither coats nor hats, nor shirts, nor shoes. Their feet and their legs froze until they were black, and it was often necessary to amputate them." Many men died of typhus, small pox, or dysentery. Although most estimates differ, some claim that as many as 3,000 soldiers died during the winter of 1777 to 1778.

A Continental soldier is pictured in this hand-colored engraving during the winter of 1777 to 1778. The morale of the patriots held out over the six-month period, especially when the Prussian soldier Baron Fredrick William von Steuben helped General Washington retrain his men. Ample food, ammunition, and new French-made uniforms also boosted spirits.

The second three months of the stay at Valley Forge improved. By March, food and supplies were finally arriving by wagon. Seventy bakers from Philadelphia came to bake bread and would take no money for their patriotic services. More important to the success of the army was the arrival of Baron Frederick William von Steuben. The baron was a Prussian captain of Frederick the Great's army. He spoke no English, but he did speak French, so Washington appointed him two French-speaking aides.

Von Steuben had arrived to train the army and quickly became popular with the men. The soldiers liked the way he demonstrated everything to them first before asking them to try it. He broke down their duties into simple steps that could be learned easily. They also liked his gruff but fair manner. Von Steuben wrote an army training manual and began using its techniques with 100 men. After he had trained these men, he sent them out to train others. Soon, larger groups were able to train together.

The increase in the troops' competency and morale was obvious within weeks. The news that France had joined the war further raised the army's spirits. Soon, French supplies and French-made uniforms arrived at camp. By May 1778, the morale at Valley Forge was high.

The news became celebratory in June when it was learned that the British had evacuated Philadelphia. The American capital was once more under American control. Later that month, on June 27 and 28, the Americans and British fought to a standstill in New Jersey at the Battle of Monmouth.

CHAPTER FOUR
The War on the Frontier

The Revolutionary War also involved actions outside of major cities like Philadelphia and New York. Some of the most brutal events of the war happened in the West. Conflict on the frontier took place between 1778 and 1779.

Many Native Americans living in the unsettled frontier regions of America allied themselves with the British. They were angry with the American colonists for settling their lands. The Native Americans felt that since the British were not after their land, they would join the British cause. Although King George had forbidden encroachment over the Appalachian Mountains in 1763, American settlers ignored his decree. By 1777, the tribes that formed the Iroquois Confederacy (the Mohawks, Oneidas,

This map illustrates the positions of the thirteen original colonies as well as other British, French, and Spanish possessions during the time before the American Revolution. Although each nation had an interest in colonizing North America, France gave up most of its territory to Great Britain after the French and Indian War (1754–1763), while other territories were ceded to, or purchased by, the United States between roughly 1700 and 1850.

Onondagas, Cayugas, and Senecas), who were at first neutral, decided to support the British.

But also in 1777, a particular event helped rally American support in the frontier settlements. Native Americans had taken two women captive and one had been killed and scalped. This tragedy caused turmoil because both women had been Loyalists. The survivor was the cousin of a British general and the dead woman was the fiancée of a British officer. News spread quickly that the British couldn't even protect their own women against their Native American allies. Soon volunteers flocked to join the American cause.

American Losses

In May 1778, a party of Loyalists and Native Americans raided Cobuskill (also known as Cobus Kill and Cobleskill), an American settlement in New York. Joseph Brant, a Mohawk chief who had once been to England and met King George, led the Native Americans. Local militia fought alongside the Indian attackers and most of the settlement was destroyed. In July, British soldiers and their Native American allies invaded settlements in Wyoming Valley, Pennsylvania. Against this force of 1,200, the Americans could send only 300 soldiers, most of them elderly men and boys. The American force was easily overcome. The Wyoming settlements were burned to the ground. Many of the settlement's residents were slaughtered.

In November of that year, more Loyalists and Native Americans invaded Cherry Valley and killed American men, women, and children. Many others were imprisoned. Again, their settlements were burned.

These events, referred to as the Wyoming Valley Massacre and the Cherry Valley Massacre, invited a brutal response from the Americans. In the spring of 1779, General Washington gave command over the counteroffensive to General John Sullivan. Sullivan's campaign quickly defeated a combined army of Loyalists and Native Americans. His troops then proceeded to lay waste to the countryside. His men chopped down orchards, burned fields, and destroyed villages. But the British and their allies were only set back, not defeated. Two more years of skirmishes and indecisive battles followed before it seemed as though the Americans had gained the upper hand.

But there was no decisive victory. Kentuckians were massacred at Blue Licks in August 1782. An American attack on Fort Oswego in

In this 1866 engraving, British sympathizers previously forced out of Wyoming Valley, Pennsylvania, return with British and Native American allies to seek revenge on colonists during the Revolutionary War. Some Native Americans, especially members of the Shawnee and Cherokee tribes, periodically attacked Americans throughout the East Coast, though the majority of them remained neutral.

New York in February 1783 also failed. Even after the war had ended, the British continued to supply the Native Americans. The war on the frontier continued for many more years.

British Losses

The British did suffer great losses along the frontier at the hands of George Rogers Clark, a Virginia explorer and older brother of William Clark, who would later lead the Corps of Discovery expedition with Meriwether Lewis. In 1777, George Rogers Clark came up with the idea of defeating the British in the Illinois Territory. He convinced Patrick Henry, the governor of Virginia, to help him with money and permission to raise troops. By June 1778, Clark had a small force of 175 men. He led them to Kaskaskia, Illinois, where on July 4, they occupied the town without a shot being fired. The women of the town begged Clark to let them see their men one more time, assuming that they would be taken prisoner or killed. Instead, Clark offered the men "all the privileges of American citizenship." They were overjoyed.

The townspeople were French citizens who had not been told about France's alliance with the United States by their British overlords. Once Clark proved to them that France and the United States were allied in their efforts to defeat Great Britain, the people of Kaskaskia became steadfast American supporters.

The priest of Kaskaskia was sent to Vincennes to report the event and acquire the allegiance of its people to Clark rather than to the British. The people of Vincennes agreed. However, once word reached Detroit about Clark's expedition, British commander Henry Hamilton launched an expedition of his own and retook Vincennes on December 17.

Hamilton decided not to attack Kaskaskia until spring. He sent his Native

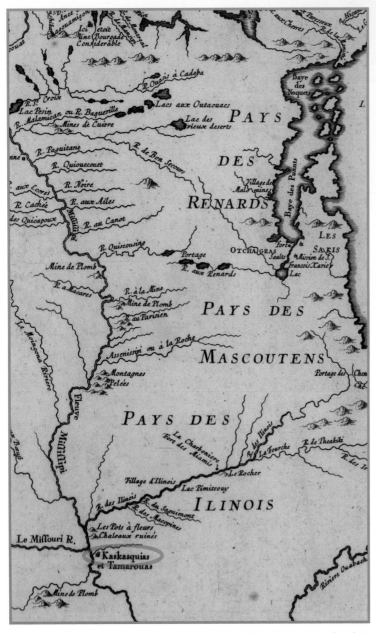

Jacques Nicolas Bellin created this map that shows Kaskaskia (spelled *Kaskasquias*), a town and British outpost in the Illinois Territory, which is circled on this detail of a map of New France. The map was created to illustrate the North American territories owned by France long before the British colonized territory near the Mississippi River. With the support of local Frenchmen from Kaskaskia, George Rogers Clark saved the frontier from defeat at the hands of the British.

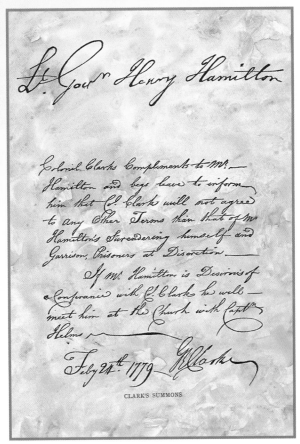

CLARK'S SUMMONS

George Rogers Clark is pictured in this dramatic painting *(left)* that depicts French citizens in the Illinois Territory fighting for the patriot cause after learning of France's alliance with the colonists against Great Britain. Clark's army took Kaskaskia on July 4, 1778, and soon after, gained control of nearby Cahokia and Vincennes. Later, the British commander Henry Hamilton recaptured Vincennes, so Clark returned to claim it again in 1779. Clark's handwritten demand for its surrender by Hamilton is pictured *(right)*.

American allies home and waited for warmer weather. Clark took advantage of the situation and with fewer than 200 men (half of them French volunteers from Kaskaskia) marched to Vincennes in February 1779. On February 25, Hamilton surrendered. The British never regained their possessions in the area and withdrew from Detroit. For the first time, American territory west of the Appalachians stretched from the Gulf of Mexico to the Great Lakes. Later, Clark would be remembered for settling these affairs diplomatically. Even the Native Americans referred to him as "the first man living, the great and invincible long-knife."

CHAPTER FIVE
The War on the Sea

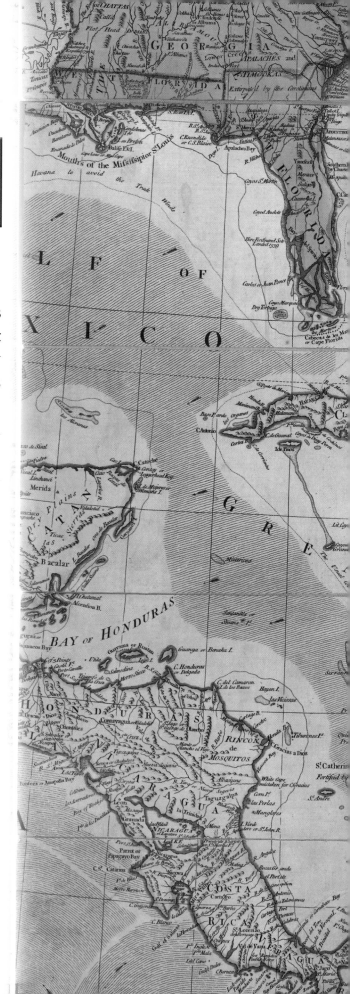

The Continental Congress was aware that the British had the finest navy in the world. They also knew they would have to deal with naval forces if they wished to win the war.

In October 1775, Congress approved funds to be used to build a small fleet. The fleet would be under the command of Commodore Esek Hopkins. By mid-February 1776, the new fleet was ready to strike. The first target was a store of gunpowder located in Nassau in the Bahamas. The powder was captured on March 3, and the fleet was able to bring its booty back to the United States. Only one month later, the small American fleet captured its first British vessel. These early successes kept spirits high.

The job of the navy was not to directly engage the British fleet, but to randomly

British mapmaker Carington Bowles created this map of North America and the West Indies in 1774. With the support of their French, Spanish, and Dutch allies, Americans were able to fight the powerful British navy, though their own sailors did little more than act as privateers. In this capacity, Americans disrupted British shipping on the high seas and captured as many as 1,200 British sailors.

attack British vessels. Great Britain had many fine ships, experienced crews, and excellent captains. The Americans' aim was to attack merchant ships transporting troops and supplies to North America. Battles with British warships were evaded whenever possible, though not all could be avoided.

John Paul Jones, in command of the American ship *Ranger*, captured the British warship *Drake* in April 1778. The next year, the king of France gave Jones a ship that he christened *Bonhomme Richard*. That September, Jones fought a battle in the *Bonhomme Richard* with the British ship *Serapis* off the coast of England. Though Jones's ship was heavily damaged, he refused to surrender. He said, "I have not yet begun to fight."

Jones captured the *Serapis*. The battle was not a complete success, though, since the *Bonhomme Richard* sank and the rest of the British ships escaped. But even a small American victory was important, especially because it occurred within sight of England's shores. Jones immediately became a hero.

American naval officer and hero John Paul Jones (1747–1792), remembered for his victory over the British in 1779, was born in Scotland. He went to sea at the age of thirteen and received his first command at the age of twenty-one. After the war, Jones went to Russia to serve as rear admiral for Catherine the Great. He died in Paris, but his remains were exhumed in 1905. They were then returned to the United States, where they now rest in a crypt at the U.S. Naval Academy Chapel in Annapolis, Maryland.

Das merckwürdige See Gefecht zwischen Capitain Pearson und Paul Jones welches 1779 den 22 September sich eraugnet wo der Cap: das Schiff den Serapis und der Paul Jones den guten Mann Richard venänt commandirte

Combat memorable entre le Pearson et Paul Jones donné le 22 7bre 1779 le Capitaine Pearson comendant le SERAPIS et Paul Jones commandant le Bon home Richart et son Escadre

This French etching depicts the Revolutionary War naval battle between John Paul Jones of the *Bonhomme Richard* and Captain Richard Pearson of the British vessel *Serapis* on September 22, 1779. Although gaining the *Serapis* was a small victory, it nevertheless boosted American morale since the capture occurred within the sight of nearby British shores.

The Americans had the will to fight on the sea but lacked enough ships and sailors. However, they had help. In 1779, Spain declared war on Great Britain, and in 1780, the Netherlands followed. Both of these countries employed their fleets against the British, keeping them busy in the Atlantic Ocean and around the world. Spain, for instance, wanted to recapture Gibraltar, a port city in southern Spain that borders

The American naval force was new and had few sailors and ships. (In 1776, the Continental navy had roughly 27 ships compared to the British naval fleet of 270 vessels.) Because of the navy's small size, recruiters were placed throughout the colonies to help hire American privateers. Colonists in New London, Connecticut, are pictured in this illustration of a local naval recruiting office.

the Strait of Gibraltar, which links the Mediterranean Sea and the North Atlantic. To ensure that Great Britain retained this land, the British had to commit at least some of their vast fleet to the Mediterranean region.

Since America's navy was so small, Americans made use of privateers who were hired to fight against the British at sea. Privateers were similar to pirates, except that they were hired and paid by a particular government to attack ships that belonged to enemies of that government. Privateers greatly expanded the ability of the Americans to inflict costly damage to the British shipping industry. Perhaps most important, the French committed their fleet to the war after their treaty with the United States was finalized. If not for the French fleet, the end of the war might have been very different.

The British attempted to invade the southern states in June 1776. The largest city in the South, Charleston, South Carolina, was their obvious target. Only a small wooden fort on nearby Sullivan Island protected Charleston. Knowing the city lacked a sophisticated defense, British general Henry Clinton expected an easy victory. Clinton planned to use his ship's guns to attack the island fort, then wade with his men across the shallow inlet to capture the island. Unprotected Charleston would then be under British control.

The Capture of Charleston

Everything went wrong with Clinton's plan. The fort's logs absorbed the impact of the cannon balls. The shallow water turned out to be more than 7 feet (2.1 m) deep. And the Americans, though under fire from British cannon, maintained return fire of their own. Realizing the city was harder to capture than he had previously thought, Clinton and his troops abandoned their mission, but only for a time.

In February 1780, the British tried to capture Charleston again, this time with nearly 14,000 soldiers and sailors. They landed 30 miles (42 km) from Charleston and slowly marched toward the city. The

The British siege of Charleston, South Carolina, which took place in the spring of 1780, is recreated in this painting. By digging trenches and inching ever closer to the city's walls, the British soldiers under General Sir Henry Clinton surrounded the city. Both the Americans and the British exchanged gunfire, and many of Charleston's wooden buildings were razed. Eventually, on May 12, 1780, the Americans under General Benjamin Lincoln surrendered.

British advance was so slow, in fact, that the Americans had time to prepare a defense. However, with little hope of reinforcements or replacement ammunition, Charleston was doomed.

The British did not reach the city until the end of March. Without hope of victory, Charleston held out until May 12, when the last American troops surrendered. The Americans suffered 240 casualties, but with 5,400 made prisoners of war, the army in South Carolina was destroyed. Considering the war in the South effectively over, Clinton returned to New York, leaving General Cornwallis, and 8,300 men, in control of the war in the southern states.

After their victory, the British established outposts around South Carolina. The last Continental army unit in South Carolina that remained intact was massacred on May 29 at Waxhaws by the forces of Lieutenant

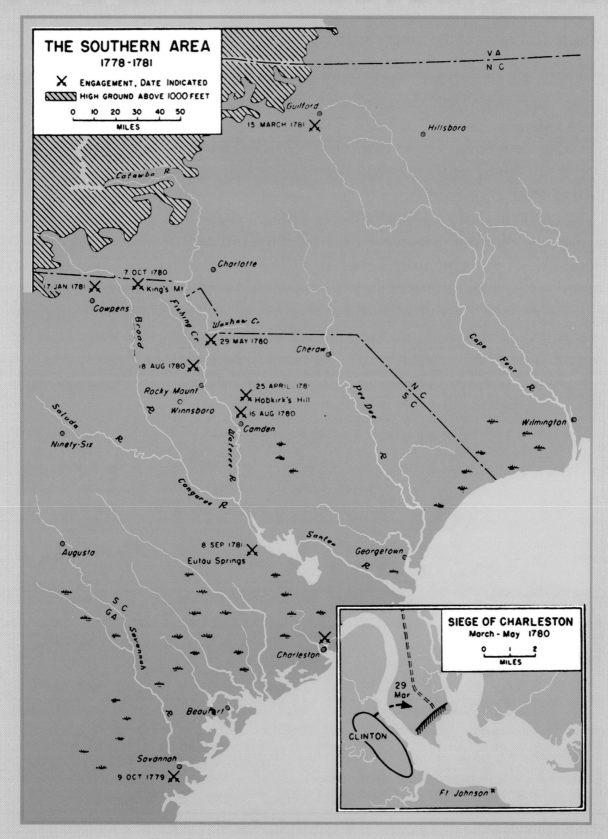

THE SOUTHERN AREA
1778-1781

✗   ENGAGEMENT, DATE INDICATED

▨   HIGH GROUND ABOVE 1000 FEET

0   10   20   30   40   50
MILES

VA
NC

Guilford

Hillsboro

15 MARCH 1781 ✗

Catawba R.

Charlotte

7 OCT 1780
17 JAN 1781 ✗   ✗ King's Mt.

Cowpens

Fishing Cr.

Broad R.

Waxhaw Cr.
✗ 29 MAY 1780

Cherow

Cape Fear R.

18 AUG 1780 ✗

25 APRIL 1781
✗ Hobkirk's Hill
✗ 16 AUG 1780

Pee Dee R.

NC
SC

Wilmington

Rocky Mount
Winnsboro
Camden

Saluda R.

Wateree R.

Ninety-Six

Congaree R.

Santee

8 SEP 1781 ✗
Eutau Springs

Georgetown R.

Augusta

SC
GA

Savannah R.

✗ Charleston

SIEGE OF CHARLESTON
March - May 1780

0   1   2
MILES

29 Mar

CLINTON

Beaufort R.

Ft. Johnson

Savannah
9 OCT 1779 ✗

This map depicts the theater of war in the southern colonies during the American Revolution, including the siege of Charleston by British troops in 1780. Obtaining control of Charleston was an important British victory: After defeating the Americans in 1780, all of the southern colonies remained under British control until the end of the war.

Colonel Banastre Tarleton. Even those men who had surrendered were killed.

Occupying South Carolina turned out to be more difficult than the British had thought. Patriots and Loyalists often clashed. Many of these situations did not involve British troops; the arguments were between Americans. Small unofficial units of patriots remained active at all times, spreading confusion among the British whenever possible. These small units were constantly on the move and difficult to track or capture.

The Battle of Camden

In North Carolina, the Americans eventually gathered troops of 1,400 men made up of recruits from Maryland and Delaware regiments. Congress sent General Horatio Gates, who was credited with the American success at Saratoga, to command them. Gates ignored the advice of men who knew the countryside and

Yet another British victory in South Carolina occurred in 1780 during the Battle of Camden. British victories in the South were a crushing blow to patriot soldiers, who were already weakened by starvation and disease. Approximately 1,000 Americans were killed or wounded during the strike, which occurred on August 16, 1780. This engraving, copied from a painting done by Alonzo Chappel, depicts the death of Continental army commander Baron Johannes de Kalb.

ended up in places where his men could find nothing to eat. The troops became sick after eating green corn, and all were exhausted from hunger and the long march.

Gates ordered a night march and finally chose a battleground where his troops were protected on both sides by swamp water. He then forced them to meet the British soldiers head-on. Although the Americans outnumbered the British, the British troops were composed of war veterans, with only a small voluntary militia. Most of the Americans, by contrast, were untrained, inexperienced men who had never been in battle.

The American militia turned and ran immediately, leaving the few Continental army units alone on the field. Even Gates fled as quickly as he could. The Continental army commanders, Johannes de Kalb and Mordecai Gist, aware of Gates's departure, put up a fight. Their men fought well, but their inexperienced 1,400 troops (plus a militia of 2,000) were no match for 2,200 well-rested, well-trained, and well-supplied British soldiers. Few Americans escaped.

The Battle of Camden was the worst defeat suffered by the American army on the field. Fatalities on the British side were 324, while the Americans suffered casualties in excess of 2,000. Many American militia units disappeared on that day, most likely returning to their homes. Their losses increased the American list of killed, wounded, captured, or deserted.

The Battle of Kings Mountain

Meanwhile, in the South, one detachment of Cornwallis's British army was moving independently of his troops' advance into North Carolina. This group, led by Major Patrick Ferguson, did not expect to meet much resistance, especially after the spectacular British success at the Battle of Camden. However, Ferguson made several mistakes. One of them was to send a taunting note to American colonel Isaac Shelby, demanding his surrender. Cornwallis threatened to come over the mountains and put him to death and burn his whole country.

Shelby was a fiercely independent frontiersman. He lived on the western side of the Appalachian Mountains in Tennessee in defiance of King George's decree that forbid such settlements. These "over-the-mountain" men were not accustomed to being told what to do. They did not look kindly upon Ferguson's threat. Shelby and 500 men headed east to meet the

Isaac Shelby (1750–1826) was born in Maryland. During the war, he provided the boats for George Rogers Clark's Illinois campaign. The North Carolina legislature awarded him with a sword for his service at Kings Mountain. After the war, he served as the first governor of Kentucky. Congress later presented him with a medal for his service in Canada at the Battle of the Thames in 1813.

would be in charge, they had a council each night to decide the next day's strategy. All agreed to hunt down Ferguson's troops.

On September 27, Ferguson heard he was being pursued. He began searching for a place for battle that would be most favorable for the British soldiers. Ferguson looked for reinforcements from local Loyalists, but he was so unpopular that none could be found. Finally, Ferguson realized that he and his troops were on their own. Time was running out. He retreated to the summit of Kings Mountain in South Carolina and prepared to fight. Because Ferguson assumed the slopes of the mountain were too steep for an attacker to overcome, he did not fortify the top of the mountain.

The steep slopes of Kings Mountain did not daunt Shelby and

British. Although most of them were illiterate and few, if any, had heard about the Declaration of Independence, they hated the British. They were willing to fight for an independent nation.

Shelby's men met with other units, some from Virginia, and others from the Carolinas. Since the leaders of these various units could not decide who

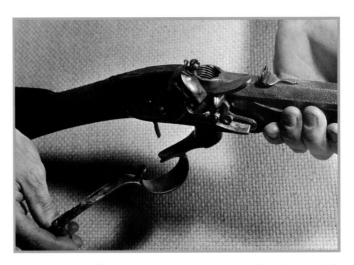

This style of flintlock musket was used by the British military in the American Revolutionary War.

his men. They had recently learned of the American massacre at Waxhaws and were eager to spill British blood. Looking for revenge, they rode all night through a rainstorm to reach Kings Mountain on October 7.

The Americans did not plan a coordinated attack but crept up the mountain slowly, each soldier moving from one tree to another. They suffered few casualties during the climb and remained strong for the fight at the summit. British bayonets drove the Americans off the summit no less than four times. But the Americans were hearty, and on the fifth assault, they killed Ferguson, and the British attempted to surrender.

But Shelby's frontiersmen refused to accept a British surrender knowing that unarmed Americans had been massacred at Waxhaws. Eventually, though, the American commanders controlled their enraged men and the hour-long battle subsided. Twenty-eight Americans were killed in the conflict and 62 were left wounded. The British losses were much greater, with 157 men dead, 167 wounded, and 698

Patriot forces raise the flag of South Carolina after fighting off the British during the Battle of Fort Moultrie in 1776. Although it was an early southern battle during the American Revolution, General William Moultrie, for whom the fort was later named, defended it from the British but later, in 1780, Fort Moultrie was defeated in the siege of Charleston.

captured. The wounded were left to die or recover.

British Setbacks

As soon as the shooting was over, the "over-the-mountain" men returned home. Cornwallis, however, remained unaware of this fact. He believed the frontiersmen were still out there, waiting to attack his men. The unwelcome news of an American victory at Kings Mountain caused him to abandon his push into North Carolina. Together with other American victories, the Battle of Kings Mountain represented the strong will of the Americans, especially frontiersmen fighting to protect land that they considered their own.

Illness, including malaria, also struck and weakened many British officers by 1780. Both Cornwallis and Tarleton were ill during this period. While the generals recovered, other officers died from widespread disease. Camden had been a spectacular victory, but Cornwallis was unable to continue his domination of the war. Between his recent defeat and the spread of disease, Cornwallis concluded that the fighting was over for the season. He established winter quarters and waited.

CHAPTER SEVEN
The World Turned Upside Down

Gates's flight during the Battle of Camden forced General Washington to appoint a more competent commander of the Continental army in the South: Nathanael Greene. Raised a Quaker, and therefore a pacifist, Greene had abandoned his religion in 1773, claiming that fighting a war to overturn injustice was a moral choice.

Greene was alarmed by the state of the American forces in South Carolina. Most people fighting in the South had begun to plunder one another. The troops lacked even the most basic necessities, such as food, clothing, and blankets. And Greene was well aware of his other challenges: any commander who had divided his forces in the war had met with disaster. When General Washington had separated his forces at New York, the British had overwhelmed him. When the British had divided their forces in New Jersey, General Washington had beaten them in Trenton. Most recently, Cornwallis had allowed Ferguson to command separate troops, and that choice ended in Ferguson's death and defeat.

Although Greene's plan to divide his already tiny army seemed like suicide, he was clever and had good reasons for his decision. One reason was that his starving, half-clothed army would then have two areas in which to forage for food. Another was that by placing

Nathanael Greene (1742–1786) had little formal education but learned a great deal on his own from books. During the early years of the war, Greene served with George Washington, whom he respected greatly. The respect was mutual, with Washington considering Greene the best candidate to take his place should he die before the war ended. After the war, he moved to Georgia, where he died a few years later from a stroke.

thought was an indefensible position. But the battle was carefully planned. The British were accustomed to American militia that fled direct attack, so when they fell back, the British soldiers thought their victory was within reach. But they were wrong. Morgan had carefully planned the retreat as a trick to make the British drop their guard. At a designated point, the retreating militia returned and continued fighting. Their British opponents, who had by now broken ranks, were stunned. Their foes were not beaten but rather

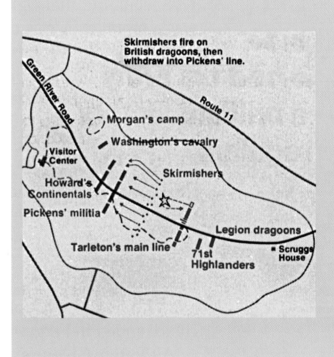

men both north and south of Cornwallis, the British general could not leave Charleston without exposing the rear of his army to attack. As long as Cornwallis remained in Charleston, he was vulnerable to attack from two directions by Americans using guerrilla warfare.

The Battle of Cowpens

On January 17, 1781, Daniel Morgan, commanding one half of Greene's army, placed his men in what he

These three maps (above and adjacent page) represent an important American victory in the South. Continental forces led by Nathanael Green and Daniel Morgan were divided in order to allow them a better opportunity to provide food for themselves and to overwhelm British forces in battle.

had lured them into a trap. At this moment, the American cavalry, hidden behind a hill, charged through the British flank and rear.

The Battle of Cowpens was a great achievement for the Americans. Ninety percent of the British force was killed or captured while twelve Americans died. General Tarleton escaped, but his forces were destroyed. In a single day, nearly one-third of Cornwallis's total manpower was gone.

Cornwallis waited 25 miles (35 km) away from Cowpens expecting news of Tarleton's victory. Instead, the news he received was tragic. He realized the Americans were far more mobile than his troops were, so he ordered his men to destroy all their heavy equipment. For two days, the British burned their own wagons and equipment, salvaging only what they could use to further their attack. Then they began their pursuit of Greene's forces.

The two armies finally met on March 15 at Guilford Court House. The battle became so desperate for the British that Cornwallis ordered

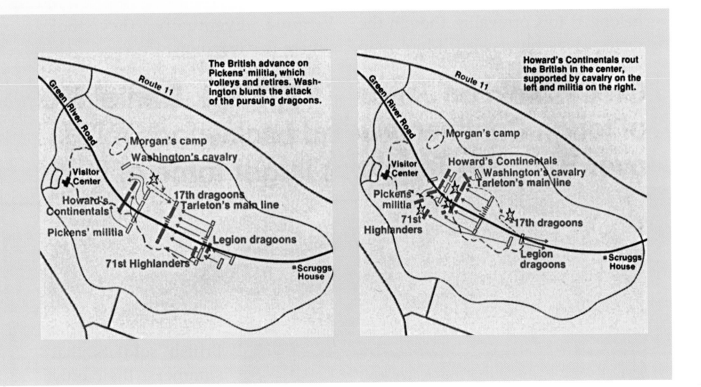

Expecting an easy victory, British forces threaten patriot militia in the first advance of the Battle of Cowpens. While British soldiers must have thought their victory was in sight, they had no idea that a surprise attack by the Continental army awaited them.

The Continental army surrounds British troops and defeats them with little opposition on January 17, 1781. The victory slowed the British advance in the South and was called an "unexpected and severe" defeat. British general Cornwallis, now with a depleted army, would no longer be able to launch aggressive attacks.

the firing of grapeshot. (Grapeshot consisted of small balls enclosed in an explosive outer shell. Once the outer shells exploded in mid-air, the balls rained down upon friend and foe alike.) At the battle near Guilford Court House, grapeshot killed soldiers on both sides. Since most of the deaths were on the American side, they withdrew. In the meantime, Cornwallis was able to re-form his troops.

By now, Greene's militia had disappeared into the woods, and his Continental army units were ragged. He decided to retreat. The battlefield belonged to Cornwallis, though the victory was bittersweet. More than one-fourth of the British force was injured or dead. Cornwallis had lost twenty-nine officers, two of them generals, and would soon lose another general to his injuries. When Parliament heard a report of the battle, one member lamented, "Another [American] victory would destroy the British army."

Cornwallis's forces were also out of food and supplies. Their nearest supply depot was 200 miles (322 km) behind them. But instead of a retreat, Cornwallis ordered his forces forward. Without supplies or food, the remains of his army limped into Virginia. Eventually, they took refuge in Yorktown.

For the rest of the spring and summer, Greene's forces fought a series of battles with the forces Cornwallis had left behind in the Carolinas. Greene's situation was desperate, but the British were in no better shape. Tarleton wrote that, for the British soldiers that summer, "their only resources were water and the wild cattle which they found in the woods."

Men in present-day Greensboro, North Carolina, are dressed in traditional clothing to accurately reenact the Battle of Guilford Court House, which took place on March 15, 1781. The battle served as a crucial victory for the patriots of North Carolina over British troops during the Revolutionary War.

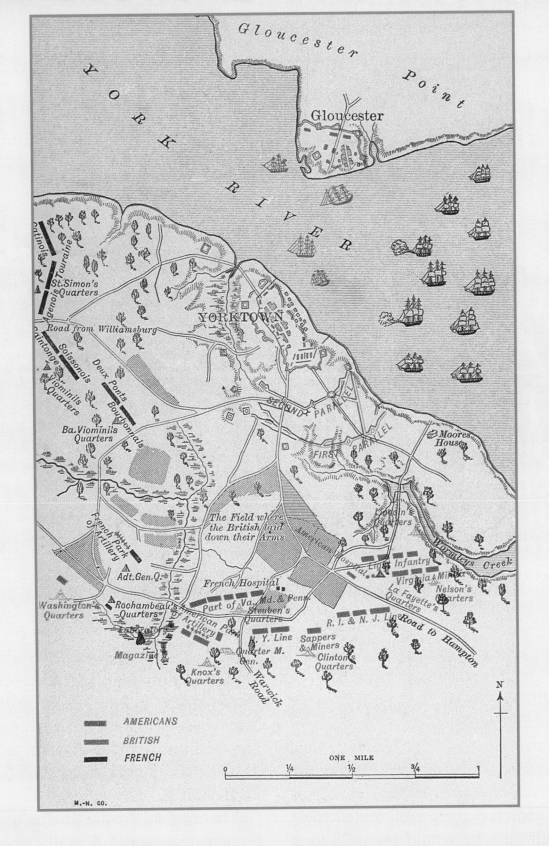

This map marks the advancements of British, American, and French troops during the Battle of Yorktown in Virginia, the last battle in the American Revolutionary War. American and French troops under General George Washington defeated what remained of the British forces on October 19, 1781.

General Cornwallis surrenders to General Washington after the British defeat at the hands of American and French forces in the Battle of Yorktown in October 1781. After several crushing blows by patriot forces, the British marched north to Virginia in order to retreat and were surrounded both on land and at sea with the help of the French. More than 8,000 British soldiers were taken prisoner at the height of the conflict.

The French naval fleet had, up until now, been of little help in the war. But on August 14, Washington received a message from the French admiral François de Grasse. De Grasse would sail for the Chesapeake Bay and stay there until mid-October. With him, he would bring 25 to 29 warships carrying 3,000 soldiers, siege guns, and mortars. Washington,

who until now had been focused on the recapture of New York, realized this was his chance. Washington marched his troops to Yorktown, and utilizing the French ships, weapons, and soldiers, set up a siege.

The British, finally realizing the French fleet would actually oppose them, sailed to Chesapeake to find the French already there. They

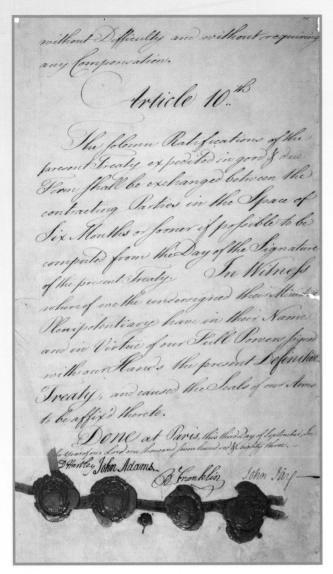

The Treaty of Paris, which was signed by officials from the American colonies and Great Britain on September 3, 1783, formally ended the Revolutionary War. Heavily negotiated with the future of the fledgling nation in mind, the patriots John Adams, Benjamin Franklin, and John Jay each took part in creating terms that allowed a fully independent United States the right to expand westward.

fought a fierce battle, the Battle of the Capes, which had no clear victor.

On September 6 and 7, the two fleets sailed south within sight of each other, but no additional battles followed. However, de Grasse knew he did not have to defeat the British. He only needed to keep them from reaching Cornwallis. Also, a smaller French fleet with supplies was currently on its way to Chesapeake. As long as de Grasse kept the British vessels busy, the smaller French fleet would not face any opposition when delivering supplies.

Cornwallis fortified his positions at Yorktown. But now he was blocked from receiving aid from the sea by the French, and a combined American and French army laid siege to him on land. Cornwallis had few options. By October 17, the British were out of ammunition and within two days, they surrendered. The British gave up their guns as their band played the song "The World Turned Upside-Down."

Isolated battles followed, mostly in frontier areas, for the next two years. But finally, on September 3, 1783, a peace treaty was signed. The British government formally recognized the independence of the United States.

CHAPTER EIGHT
After the War

The war had been won, but the peace that followed was a chaotic time. The Articles of Confederation, which Congress had adopted in 1781, were insufficient guidelines to govern the nation. The articles established a "league of friendship" between the states but did not decide issues related to commerce, taxation, and fiscal policy. The Founding Fathers knew that a lack of cooperation between the thirteen states would surely doom the fledgling nation quickly.

Congress also had a great deal of new territory to consider. Borders were disputed between the United States, Great Britain, France, and Spain, not to mention the Native Americans who lived there. Still, the United States had gained plenty of territory in the war, even if no laws were in place governing exactly how much land was gained or where it ended.

The United States, seen in this map after the signing of the Treaty of Paris in 1783, was already in the process of expansion. This idea was later known as Manifest Destiny—the belief that Americans had the God-given right to expand their nation to the Pacific Ocean. As pioneers moved west and settled in specific territories, those areas applied for statehood and established constitutions based on the needs and populations of each state.

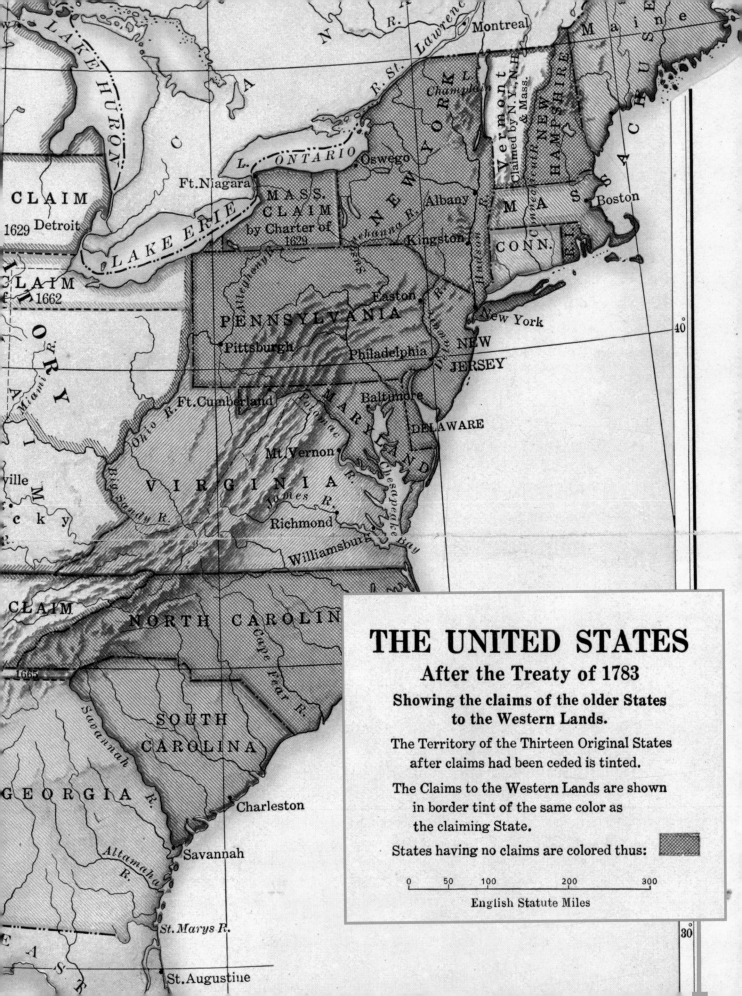

THE UNITED STATES

After the Treaty of 1783

Showing the claims of the older States to the Western Lands.

The Territory of the Thirteen Original States after claims had been ceded is tinted.

The Claims to the Western Lands are shown in border tint of the same color as the claiming State.

States having no claims are colored thus:

```
0    50   100         200        300
```

English Statute Miles

In 1784, Thomas Jefferson came up with a plan to divide the territory between the Appalachian Mountains and the Mississippi River. He wanted the territory to become several new states: Sylvania, Michigania, Cherronesus, Assenisipia, Metropotamia, Saratoga, Illinoia, Washington, Polypotamia, and Pelisipia. Congress, however, lacked any real ability to officially claim the land, survey it, or defend it, let alone name it. The plan was shelved.

Shays's Rebellion

Congress, and the country, limped along until given a wake-up call in 1786 by Shays's Rebellion. Severe economic troubles had plagued the states after the war, and the deprivations in western Massachusetts had been especially harsh. The problems were made worse by merchants refusing to accept paper money printed by Congress. They insisted instead on hard cash in the form of gold or silver coins. The farmers of Massachusetts didn't have the currency to pay their debts, and many went to jail.

A veteran of the Revolution and a farmer, Captain Daniel Shays provided the leadership the unhappy farmers needed. He led 1,500 men, many of them wearing their old army uniforms, to the Springfield Courthouse in September 1786. There they stayed, preventing the Supreme Court from meeting. In January, Shays and his followers attacked the Federal Arsenal in Springfield, which was successfully defended by local militia.

The ragtag army of farmers soon dispersed and was chased into neighboring towns. After a confrontation with militia on February 3, the farmers disbanded. The "rebellion" was over. Although few died, the inability of Congress to do anything about the reforms the farmers demanded prompted many to rethink the Articles of Confederation. Thomas Jefferson wrote, "I hold it that a little rebellion now and then is a good thing."

George Washington wrote, "Wisdom and good examples are necessary at this time to rescue the political machine from the impending storm." Jefferson and Washington were not the only ones who realized that a stronger document was desperately needed. Without one, the new

Although Americans were victorious after the Revolutionary War, life in the new nation was hardly easy. Many people struggled to survive, and the country faced a long period of economic depression. Because people without property could not vote, they felt powerless to change laws that seemed unjust. Objecting to high taxes and valueless paper money, Daniel Shays, leading a mob in this print (right), organized an uprising of 1,500 farmers in August 1786 to February 1787 that later became known as Shays's Rebellion.

country was in danger of melting away through internal strife.

On May 25, 1787, the Constitutional Convention convened at the Pennsylvania State House. Former general George Washington was elected the president of the convention. He expressed embarrassment at his lack of qualifications but promised to do his best. In fact, Washington's best qualification was that he was well-liked and trusted. The men meeting to draft a new constitution for the country were quarrelsome, opinionated, and often uninterested in compromise. They

George Washington, Benjamin Franklin, and other Founding Fathers are pictured inside Independence Hall signing the U.S. Constitution in Philadelphia, Pennsylvania. Thirty-nine delegates arrived at the Constitutional Convention in 1787 where they approved and signed the Constitution on September 17, 1787. The document was made public within days amid outcry that it represented a system of government that was too similar to the old British system.

would need someone they respected to keep them on course.

Some members of the convention thought the country needed a king. Others proposed plans for a strong central government, divided into three branches: legislative, judicial, and executive. The smaller states proposed a plan that gave more power to the states and kept a smaller, less influential central government.

After arguing for months, the convention finally requested that a committee draft the proposed constitution, which was presented on August 6, 1787. Arguments again broke out over issues like the regulation of commerce and slavery. By the end of the month, one of the delegates, George Mason, wrote his son that he "would sooner chop off [my] right hand than put it to the Constitution as it now stands."

On September 17, the convention finally agreed on the latest draft of the document. The exhausted delegates shared a farewell dinner and left for their respective homes. A series of anonymous essays began to appear, promoting the Constitution. These were referred to as the Federalist Papers and were actually written by Alexander Hamilton, John Jay, and James Madison. These eighty-five essays appeared primarily in the *New York Packet* and the *Independent Journal*. Jefferson referred to the Federalist Papers as the

Etched by Albert Rosenthal 1888.

George Mason (1725–1792) was one of the most influential minds of the American Revolution. In May 1776, he wrote a bill of rights and a constitution for Virginia, upon which Thomas Jefferson later drew his own inspiration for the original draft of the Declaration of Independence. Mason's ideas formed the first ten amendments to the Constitution, otherwise known as the Bill of Rights.

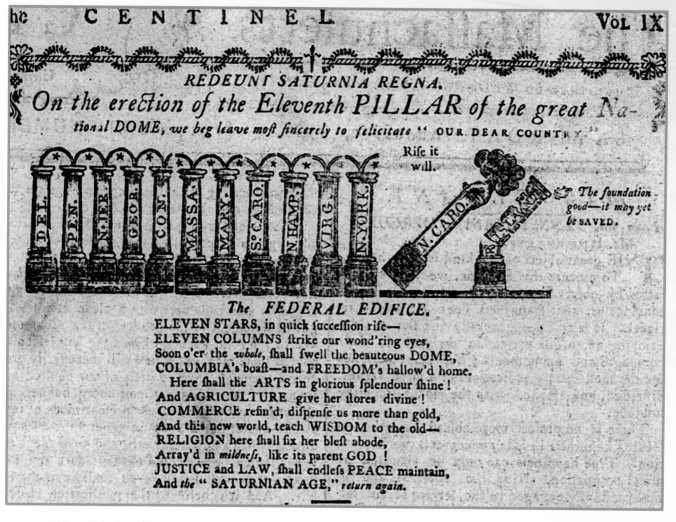

The FEDERAL EDIFICE.

ELEVEN STARS, in quick succession rise—
ELEVEN COLUMNS strike our wond'ring eyes,
Soon o'er the *whole*, shall swell the beauteous DOME,
COLUMBIA's boast—and FREEDOM's hallow'd home.
  Here shall the ARTS in glorious splendour shine!
And AGRICULTURE give her stores divine!
  COMMERCE refin'd, dispense us more than gold,
And this new world, teach WISDOM to the old—
RELIGION here shall fix her blest abode,
Array'd in *mildness*, like its parent GOD!
JUSTICE and LAW, shall endless PEACE maintain,
And *the* " SATURNIAN AGE," *return again.*

This political cartoon symbolizes the support of individual states for the union of the United States as each approved the Constitution. "The Erection of the Eleventh Pillar" was published in the *Massachusetts Centinel* in 1788.

"best commentary on the principles of government ever written."

The concluding essay of the Federalist Papers contained Hamilton's opinion: "A nation, without a national government, is, in my view, an awful spectacle. The establishment of a Constitution, in time of profound peace, by the voluntary consent of a whole people, is a prodigy, to the completion of which I look forward with trembling anxiety."

Nine states needed to ratify the Constitution before it was official. By January 1788, five states had ratified the document, but the outcome looked bleak in many of the other states.

On July 2, 1788, Congress received word that the state of New

THE FOUNDATION OF AMERICAN GOVERNMENT

This 1897 painting recreates the moment that the United States' Constitution was signed by Benjamin Franklin, as George Washington leans over to watch. More than seventy delegates were invited to attend the Constitutional Convention in Philadelphia, but only thirty-nine delegates signed the document. Franklin, at age eighty-one, was the oldest representative in attendance.

Hampshire was the ninth state to ratify the Constitution. Two more states, Virginia and New York, ratified the Constitution shortly thereafter.

Seven years after the war ended, the country had a central government, one that had the power to tax, to regulate commerce, and to raise an army, should the need arise. The dream of a United States independent from Great Britain and strong enough to stand on its own had finally been realized.

TIMELINE

1733 Parliament passes the Molasses Act.

1754–1763 French and Indian War occurs.

1763 Great Britain attempts to keep settlers from heading west.

1764 The Sugar Act and Currency Act are passed by Parliament.

1765 The Stamp Act is passed.

1766 The Stamp Act is repealed.

1767 The Townshend Duties are passed.

1770 Five people are fatally shot in an event known as the Boston Massacre.

1773 The Sons of Liberty organization is formed.

September 1774 The First Continental Congress meets in Philadelphia and advocates a boycott against British goods; adopts Declaration of Rights and Grievances.

April 1775 The Revolutionary War begins after the Battles of Lexington and Concord.

May 1775 The meeting of the Second Continental Congress; American forces capture Fort Ticonderoga in New York.

June 1775 The Battle of Bunker Hill is fought outside Boston.

March 1776 The British leave Boston.

June 1776 The British attempt to invade the southern states, beginning with Charleston, South Carolina; British troops also arrive in New York Harbor with a massive naval fleet.

July 1776 The colonies declare their independence.

August 1776 Americans defeated in Manhattan and Brooklyn.

October 1776 American defeat on Lake Champlain; Washington's troops are defeated in the Battle of White Plains.

December 1776 General Washington leads American troops to victory in Trenton, New Jersey.

January 1777 Another victory for Washington and his troops, this time in Princeton, New Jersey.

June 1777 British troops try again to invade New York from Canada.

July 1777 The Marquis de Lafayette joins the American cause and eventually becomes Washington's aide.

August 1777 Americans defeat Hessians in the Battle of Bennington.

September 1777 The British capture Philadelphia.

October 1777 Americans win the Battles of Saratoga.

November 1777 Congress adopts the Articles of Confederation.

December 1777 Continental army sets up winter quarters at Valley Forge in Pennsylvania.

February 1778 France enters the war on the side of the United States.

June 1778 Americans and British fight in the Battle of Monmouth.

July 1778 France declares war against Britain.

December 1778 The British capture Savannah, Georgia.

1779 The British leave Philadelphia; John Paul Jones defeats the *Serapis*.

February 1780 The British capture Charleston.

June 1780 American forces defeat the British in the Battle of Springfield.

1781 British general Cornwallis surrenders at Yorktown, Virginia; Congress adopts the Articles of Confederation.

September 1783 The Treaty of Paris is signed by Great Britain and the United States.

GLOSSARY

advocate One who argues for a cause.

blockade The act of using ships to block the entrance to a harbor or port, keeping a city from selling or receiving goods.

boycott To purposefully refuse to have dealings with a person, store, or organization; to refuse the traded goods of a foreign country or countries.

Declaration of Rights and Grievances A document composed by John Adams and passed by the First Continental Congress in 1774 that outlined the Americans' position toward legislation drafted by the British Parliament.

dysentery An infection of the lower intestinal tract that produces severe diarrhea.

encroachment An infringement upon the property of others.

entrenchment To place in a trench.

Hessian A German soldier paid by the British to fight for them; a mercenary.

Intolerable Acts (Coercive Acts) Legislation adopted by the British in response to the Boston Tea Party. The Intolerable Acts closed the Boston port until the tea was paid for, prohibiting all coastal trade except for food and firewood.

Loyalist A supporter of the lawful government during a revolt or revolution; Americans who supported the British during the Revolutionary War.

mercenary A soldier who is hired by a government to fight for it.

militia A military force that is not part of the regular national army; a group of volunteers.

Molasses Act A law passed in 1733 by Parliament to stop importation of foreign molasses by imposing a high prohibitive tax on it. The law was largely ignored by American colonists who continued to import molasses from the West Indies.

morale The state of mind of an individual or group in regard to confidence, cheerfulness, and discipline.

pacifist A person who is opposed to war or violence as a means of resolving disputes.

rampage A course of violent, frenzied action or behavior.

republic A government in which the head of state is usually a president elected by the people.

retreat To leave the scene of combat.

sentry A soldier who stands guard.

skirmish A minor fight in a war as opposed to a major battle.

smallpox A highly infectious viral disease characterized by high fever and pustules that form pockmarks.

stockpile A storehouse or reserve supply.

Townshend Duties Additional taxes levied in 1767 on goods such as paper, glass, and tea that were actually extensions of the existing Navigation Acts.

typhus Any of severe forms of infectious disease caused by microorganisms and characterized by severe headache, high fever, depression, delirium, and rashes.

FOR MORE INFORMATION

American Battlefield
    Protection Program
National Park Service
1201 Eye Street NW, Suite 2255
Washington, DC 20005
(202) 513-7270

National Society of the Sons of the
    American Revolution
1000 S. Fourth Street
Louisville, KY 40203
(502) 589-1776

Web Sites

Due to the changing nature of Internet links, the Rosen Publishing Group, Inc., has developed an online list of Web sites related to the subject of this book. This site is updated regularly. Please use this link to access the list:

http://www.rosenlinks.com/ushagn/amre

FOR FURTHER READING

Collins, Kathleen. *Marquis De Lafayette: French Hero of the American Revolution* (Primary Sources of Famous People in American History). New York: The Rosen Publishing Group, Inc., 2004.

Kallen, Stuart A. *Life During the American Revolution* (The Way People Live). San Diego: Lucent Books, 2003.

Masoff, Joy. *American Revolution, 1700–1800* (Chronicle of America). New York: Scholastic Reference, 2000.

Murray, Stuart. *American Revolution* (Eyewitness Books). New York: DK Publishing, 2002.

BIBLIOGRAPHY

Commager, Henry Steele, and Richard B. Morris, eds. *The Spirit of Seventy-Six: The Story of the American Revolution as Told by Participants.* New York: DeCapo Press, 1995.

Historyplace.com. "The History Place: American Revolution; An Unlikely Victory 1777–1783." Retrieved June 30, 2003 (http://www.historyplace.com/unitedstates/revolution/revwar-77.htm).

Leckie, Robert. *George Washington's War: The Saga of the American Revolution.* New York: HarperCollins, 1992.

Mitchell, Joseph B. *Decisive Battles of the American Revolution.* New York: G. P. Putnam's Sons, 1962.

Morison, Samuel Eliot, ed. *Sources and Documents Illustrating the American Revolution 1764–1788 and the Formation of the Federal Constitution.* New York: Oxford University Press, 1965.

Wood, W. J. *Battles of the Revolutionary War: 1775–1781.* Chapel Hill, NC: Algonquin Books, 1990.

INDEX

About the Author

Martha Kneib is a native St. Louisian who holds a master's degree in anthropology. She devotes most of her time to writing, maintaining her Web sites, and traveling with her husband. This is her fifth book for the Rosen Publishing Group.

Photo Credits

Cover (background), pp. 1 (background), 4–5, 8–9, 10–11, 12, 30, 32–33 courtesy of the Library of Congress, Geography and Maps Division; cover (top right), p. 14 (left) © Museum of the City of New York/Corbis; cover (bottom right) courtesy of Teaching Politics; pp. 6, 35, 50, 56, 58, 59 courtesy of the Library of Congress, Prints and Photographs Division; pp. 7, 12 (inset), 20, 29, 42 (right), 46 (top), 52–53, 57 © Hulton Archive/Getty Images; p. 13 engrossed copy of the Declaration of Independence, August 2, 1776, Miscellaneous Papers of the Continental Congress, 1774–1789, Records of the Continental and Confederation Congresses and the Constitutional Convention, 1774–1789, Record Group 360, National Archives; p. 14 (right) © The Art Archive/ Gripsholm Castle, Sweden/Dagli Orti; p. 16 © The Art Archive/John Meek; pp. 17, 19, 26–27, 39, 46–47 courtesy of the General Libraries, the University of Texas at Austin; p. 19 (inset) © Bettmann/Corbis; pp. 22–23, 25, 31 (right), 36, 38, 43, 49 © North Wind/North Wind Picture Archives; p. 31 (left) courtesy of the NARA, Pictures of the Revolutionary War, 66-G5-106; p. 34 © The Pierpont Morgan Library/Art Resource, NY; p. 40 courtesy of the NARA, Pictures of the Revolutionary War, 148-GW-164; p. 42 (left) © The Filson Historical Society; p. 48 © Gary W. Carter/Corbis; p. 51 Treaty of Paris, 1783, International Treaties and Related Records, 1778–1974, General Records of the United States Government, Record Group 11, National Archives.

Designer: Tahara Anderson; **Editor:** Joann Jovinelly